Curriculum Visions Explorers

Exploring the

Tudor Age
of
Discovery

D1549272

World history

3000 BC		2000 BC		1000 BC	

Ancient Egyptians (3000–332 BC)

Ancient Gree

Age of Discovery timeline

Prince Henry the Navigator
sends ships to find a sea
route to China.

Bartolomeu Dias sails around
the Cape of Good Hope.

Vasco da Gama
reaches India.

1420	1430	1440	1450	1460	1470	1480	1490	1500	1510

Christopher Columbus
reaches the 'New World'.

John Cabot lands
in Newfoundland.

Contents

Look up the **bold** words in the glossary
on page 32 of this book.

A small world

If you stood at Lands End on the southwestern tip of England in the Middle Ages and looked west, then you would have had no idea what lay beyond the horizon.

The great ocean to the west – the Atlantic Ocean – went on, some said, until the end of the world was reached. Then, if you sailed further, you simply fell off the edge.

You can see how much the Europeans knew of the world by looking at the map on this page. You will see other maps as you go through the book, and it will always be useful to compare them with this one.

At this time, Europeans thought that Europe, Asia and (North) Africa was surrounded by a great ocean. They did not know that America existed.

N

British Isles

This strange medieval map (Mappa Mundi) had Jerusalem at its centre and north was to the left. It was made in a monastery and Jerusalem was the most important place in their world. Turn the book around to put north uppermost. The Mediterranean Sea is coloured black and has lots of islands.

E

Q Why did early maps put Jerusalem in the middle?

Jerusalem

S

W

The Tudors explore

Peoples of countries like Spain, Portugal, Italy, France and England had to find a way to reach the silks and spices they wanted from Asia and the gold from Africa. The Muslim **Turks** would not let them go overland. The only other way to get to China and the rest of Africa was by sea.

The first peoples to look for a sea route to China (which at this time was known as Cathay) were the Portuguese. They sailed around Africa, building forts and claiming land as they went.

This meant that Spain, which was next in the race, could not go along the coast of Africa. This is why they paid Christopher Columbus to go west across the Atlantic Ocean and why he was the first European to reach the Americas.

Soon, Portugal and Spain were claiming all of these new worlds. England was losing out. These new **colonies** promised to make Spain, in particular, even more wealthy and powerful. This was something that did not please the first Tudor king, Henry VII, at all.

At this time, even a small bag of nutmeg could make a person wealthy. Tudor **merchants** and kings were very interested in having a part of, or better still, controlling, the spice, silk and gold trade. That is why England joined the discovery race.

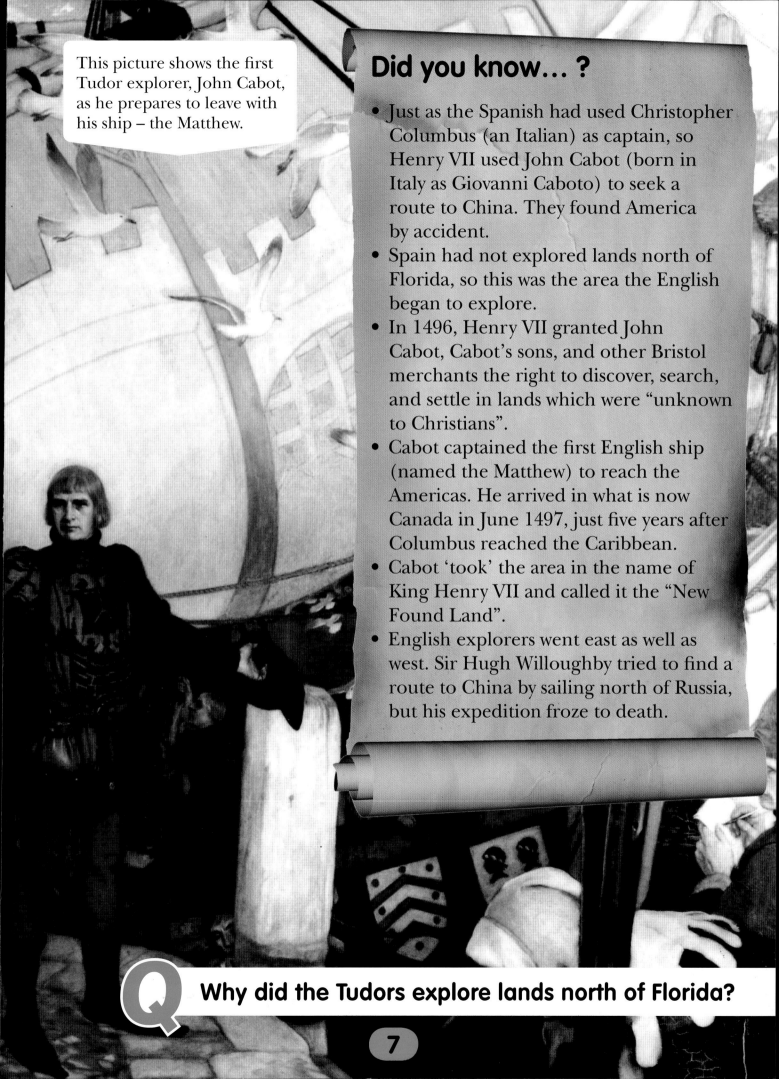

This picture shows the first Tudor explorer, John Cabot, as he prepares to leave with his ship – the Matthew.

Did you know... ?

- Just as the Spanish had used Christopher Columbus (an Italian) as captain, so Henry VII used John Cabot (born in Italy as Giovanni Caboto) to seek a route to China. They found America by accident.
- Spain had not explored lands north of Florida, so this was the area the English began to explore.
- In 1496, Henry VII granted John Cabot, Cabot's sons, and other Bristol merchants the right to discover, search, and settle in lands which were "unknown to Christians".
- Cabot captained the first English ship (named the Matthew) to reach the Americas. He arrived in what is now Canada in June 1497, just five years after Columbus reached the Caribbean.
- Cabot 'took' the area in the name of King Henry VII and called it the "New Found Land".
- English explorers went east as well as west. Sir Hugh Willoughby tried to find a route to China by sailing north of Russia, but his expedition froze to death.

Q Why did the Tudors explore lands north of Florida?

The Golden Hind

During Tudor times, ships became seaworthy enough to make an ocean voyage. The most famous English ship was called the Golden Hind. This was the ship used by Sir Francis Drake on his voyage around the world. It was typical of the ships used during the **Age of Discovery**.

The Golden Hind was a cargo ship and also a **man o'war**. By modern standards it was very small. It was 21 metres long and weighed about 100 tonnes. It had 20 officers, 60 crew, and 3 boys who acted as lookouts by climbing to the tops of the masts. The ship had 18 guns.

All ships needed **ballast** in the bottom to stop them toppling over. On the way out this ballast was made of boulders. It was hoped that, on the way back, the rocks could be replaced with treasure!

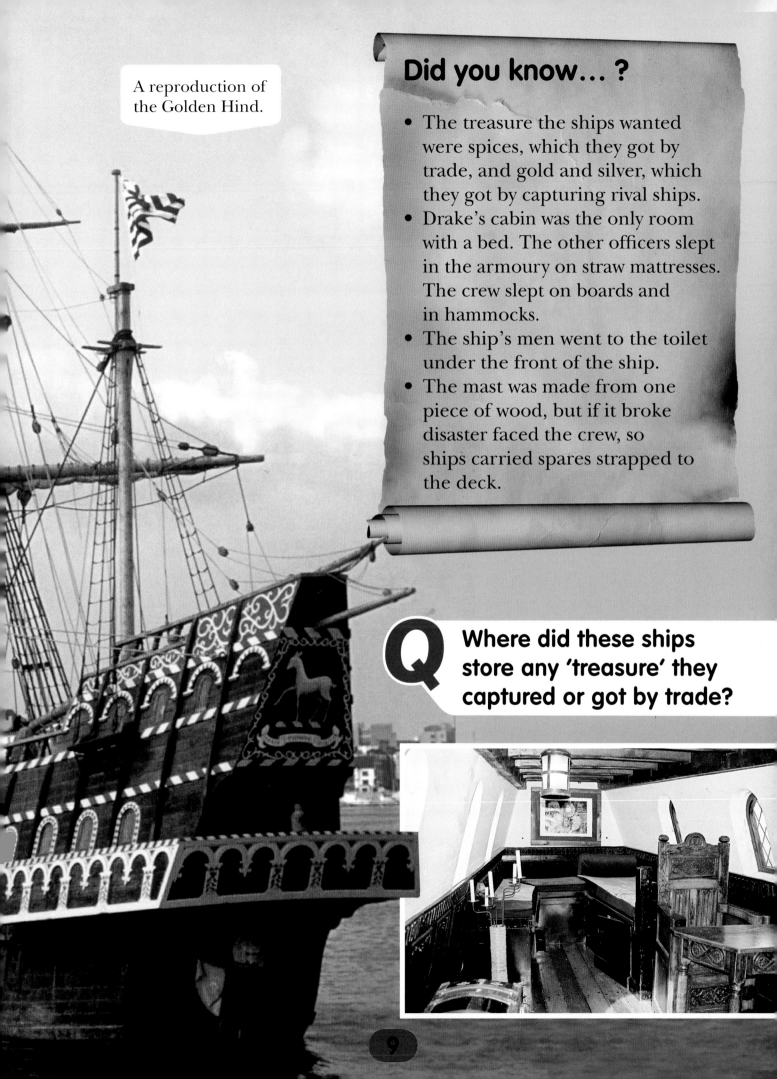

A reproduction of the Golden Hind.

Did you know... ?

- The treasure the ships wanted were spices, which they got by trade, and gold and silver, which they got by capturing rival ships.
- Drake's cabin was the only room with a bed. The other officers slept in the armoury on straw mattresses. The crew slept on boards and in hammocks.
- The ship's men went to the toilet under the front of the ship.
- The mast was made from one piece of wood, but if it broke disaster faced the crew, so ships carried spares strapped to the deck.

Q Where did these ships store any 'treasure' they captured or got by trade?

Q Which route did Drake follow to get around the world?

A 'Golden Hind' crew member dressed as Sir Francis Drake, aboard the reproduction of the original 16th century ship.

Did you know... ?

- Before he made his round the world journey Sir Francis Drake was a **privateer** (an official pirate).
- He was second-in-command of the English fleet against the Spanish Armada in 1588.
- He died of **dysentery** after unsuccessfully attacking San Juan, Puerto Rico.
- He was a hero to the English but a devil to the Spanish, who called him "El Dragón" for his privateering. King Philip II of Spain offered a ransom for him, which in today's money would be worth £5 million.

Drake's voyage of discovery

The first people to sail right around the world were the Spanish crew of the ship whose captain was Ferdinand Magellan. It took three years. They were searching for the Spice Islands (Indonesia). Magellan found a narrow channel of water (a strait) in which to cross South America into the Pacific ocean.

The second captain to sail around the world was Englishman, Sir Francis Drake. He was an adventurous man, always looking for a challenge. This was just the sort of man Queen Elizabeth I was looking for in the race to find new riches.

In 1577, Drake was sent by Queen Elizabeth to claim land along the Pacific coast of North America and stop the Spanish from getting it. It turned out to be a rather longer voyage than that.

He set out on 13 December, aboard his flagship, the Pelican (renamed Golden Hind when it reached America), together with the Elizabeth, the Marygold, the Swan and the Benedict. In all there were over 160 men.

After crossing the Atlantic, two ships became unseaworthy. The other three sailed through Magellan's Strait, but were then caught in great storms. The Marygold sank, and the Elizabeth turned back to England, so only Drake's Golden Hind continued around the world.

(*continued on next page*)

Drake completes his journey

By the time Drake reached the western shore of South America he only had one ship. He had renamed it the Golden Hind in honour of the hind (deer) on the coat of arms of the man who had given him the money for the voyage.

The Golden Hind sailed north along the Pacific coast of South America, attacking Spanish ports and capturing some Spanish ships and their treasure.

On 17 June, 1579, Drake landed somewhere in California.

Drake did not sail back home after all this adventure. Instead, he sailed west across the Pacific, and a few months later reached the Spice Islands.

He then went round the Cape of Good Hope in southern Africa, and reached Sierra Leone on 22 July, 1580. Finally, on 26 September, the Golden Hind sailed into Plymouth with Drake and 59 remaining crew, along with a rich cargo of spices and captured Spanish treasures.

Drake claimed the whole coast north of California for the English Crown and called it Nova Albion, meaning 'New Britain'.

Did you know… ?

- The Queen's half-share of Drake's cargo was worth more than the rest of her income for that entire year.
- Drake was knighted by Queen Elizabeth I aboard the Golden Hind on 4 April, 1581.
- The Queen ordered all written accounts of Drake's voyage to be classed as secret, and its crew were sworn to silence on pain of death. She wanted to keep Drake's successes secret from Spain.

Q Did Drake follow the same route as Magellan?

The journey around the world

15 Nov 1577 Left Plymouth but returned owing to bad weather.

13 Dec 1577 Left Plymouth again.

20 Jun 1578 South America, Port Julian. Thomas Doughty tried and executed for mutiny.
The ships Swan and Christopher (Benedict had been renamed Christopher) broken up as they are no longer needed. Stores and crew transferred to remaining ships. The Pelican is renamed Golden Hind.

20 Aug 1578 Enter Straits of Magellan.

6 Sep 1578 Reach Pacific.

30 Sep 1578 Marygold lost. Golden Hind and Elizabeth blown 300 miles south to Cape Horn.

7 Oct 1578 Violent squall separates Golden Hind and Elizabeth. Elizabeth returns home.

5 Dec 1578 Raid on Valparaiso. Capture Spanish ship carrying gold and wines. Ship refitted.

1 Mar 1579 Capture of the Cacafuego. Treasure: 80lb gold, 13 chests of pieces of eight, 26 tons of silver, jewels and pearls.

15 Apr 1579 Reach Central America.

Drake's route shown on an old map.

1 Jun 1579	Latitude 48°N reached. North West route considered too great a hazard. Return to Nova Albion.
23 Jul 1579	Left Nova Albion.
16 Oct 1579	Reached Philippines.
3 Nov 1579	Reached Spice Islands (Indonesia). Trade agreement made with Sultan of Ternate. 6 tons of cloves taken aboard.
9 Jan 1580	Ship strikes a reef; 8 cannon and 3 tons of cloves jettisoned. Wind changed and ship slid off reef.
26 Mar 1580	Reached Java and left for Cape of Good Hope.
22 July 1580	Reached Sierra Leone.
26 Sep 1580	Return to Plymouth.

Meeting the Inuit

The English were convinced there ought to be a way around the north of America just as there was a way around the south. They called this northern route the Northwest Passage.

Martin Frobisher left England in 1576 and reached the cold lands of Baffin Island, Canada. There he came across some native peoples – the Inuit (Eskimos) in their **kayaks** who were making their way to their summer hunting grounds.

The Inuit were amazed to see the English in their ship and paddled out to Frobisher's ship.

The Inuits offered trade, but during the time of trading some of Frobisher's men went ashore, wandered out of sight and could not be found. Frobisher mistakenly thought his men had been captured so he took an Inuit captive and sailed back to England. The crew on land were now abandoned, although they had not been harmed. Thus the first contact in the north began with a misunderstanding and it would not be the last.

On the second journey more misunderstandings led to a fight. That is what this picture shows.

The second meeting between Frobisher and the Inuit.

Did you know... ?

- Frobisher was looking for treasure and had miners with him.
- The miners mistook the worthless mineral called iron pyrites (fool's gold) for real gold and took a ship load back to England.
- Frobisher wanted to start a mining colony but he did not have the supplies to do so. As a result, he did not start the first colony in northern America.

Q What went wrong when Frobisher met the Inuit?

Privateers

By the time Queen Elizabeth I came to the throne, Spain was getting enormous amounts of gold and silver from her new colonies.

Elizabeth wanted a share of this wealth but most of her explorers (except Drake) were not very successful in finding riches. So she agreed that some of England's best sailors could be **privateers**, effectively official pirates.

They would go off, funded by London or Bristol merchants, and capture the Spanish and Portuguese treasure ships – if they could. The places where they attacked the Spanish ships were the areas close to the Caribbean and the Spanish ports. This was called the **Spanish Main**.

Spain started a system of **convoys** to protect itself from the privateers. Even so, privateers brought much needed gold and silver to England.

The most famous British privateer was Sir Francis Drake. However, Captain Christopher Newport led more attacks than any other English privateer. In 1592, Newport captured the Portuguese ship, Madre de Dios. His men collected five hundred tons of spices, silks, gemstones and other treasures. It was the most valuable prize captured during Elizabethan privateering times.

Did you know… ?

- Privateers brought **booty** from their raids and helped to turn England – and London in particular – into a centre of trade.
- Elizabethan palaces such as Longleat, Wollaton and Hardwick, are among the biggest palaces ever built in England. They were all built from the wealth of Tudor trade.

A meeting between English and Spanish ships.

Q Who was the most famous privateer?

Roanoke, the first English settlement

In Tudor times, the challenge of setting up a **colony** far away across a great ocean was enormous. The person most keen on starting a colony was Sir Walter Raleigh.

The queen also wanted a base from which her privateers could attack the Spanish fleets. So in 1584 she allowed Raleigh to form a settlers expedition of two small boats, led by Philip Amadas and Arthur Barlowe.

The expedition arrived at the sheltered site they called Roanoke. Here they met the Native Americans who lived in the area. The native peoples and the settlers traded: leather, coral, dyes and much more in exchange for hatchets, axes and knives. In September, two Native Americans – Manteo and Wanchese – agreed to go back to England with the expedition.

The arrival of trade goods and the Native Americans, made people in England even more enthusiastic about colonising the Americas. Raleigh named the place the expedition had visited Virginia, in honour of the Virgin Queen Elizabeth I.

The first settlers' ships landed in what is now North Carolina, USA.

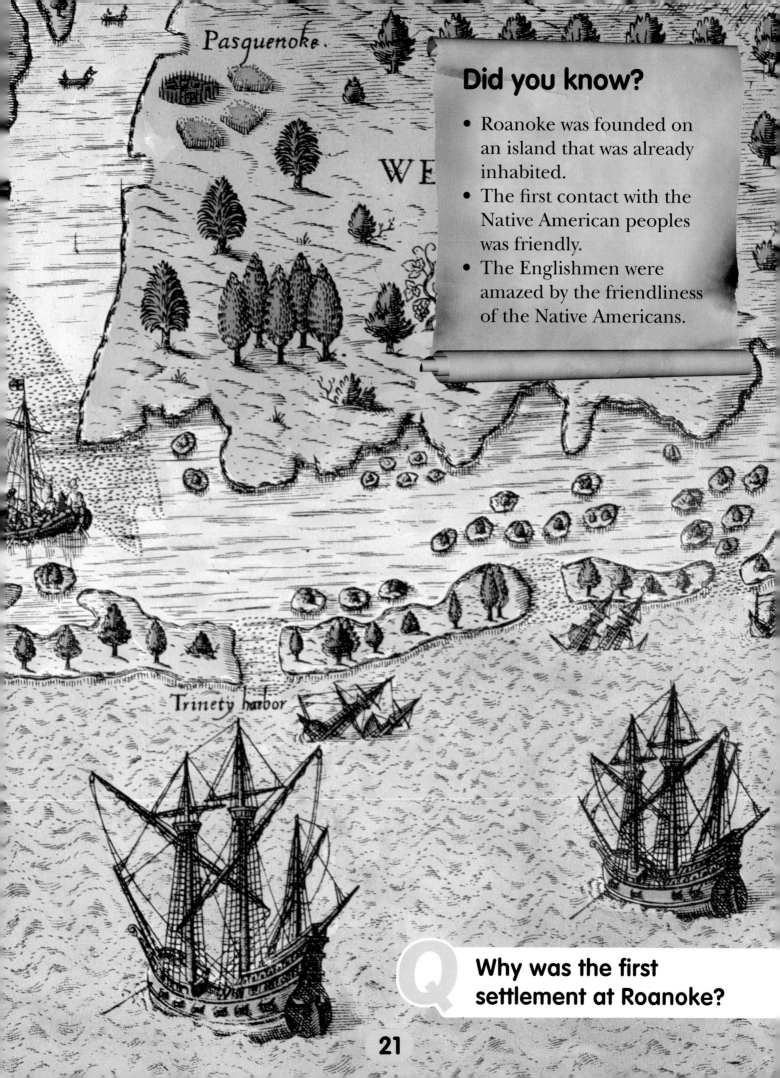

Pasquenoke.

WE

Trinety harbor

Did you know?

- Roanoke was founded on an island that was already inhabited.
- The first contact with the Native American peoples was friendly.
- The Englishmen were amazed by the friendliness of the Native Americans.

Q **Why was the first settlement at Roanoke?**

The Native Americans

In 1585, Raleigh organised a second voyage, this time to take 300 colonists to Roanoke Island in seven ships.

However, over the coming months, relations became strained as the English wanted to trade for more and more food. This made the Native Americans short of supplies for they only grew enough for their own needs. However, the English did not realise this.

With too little food to go around, relations with the local native peoples got worse. Some Native Americans wanted to get rid of the English, but the colonists learned of this. With the words "Christ our Victory" as the signal, the colonists attacked the village and beheaded the chief.

Without the goodwill of the Native Americans, the colonists now had a very hard time finding enough food, since they were not familiar with the plants and animals around them. Eventually they were rescued by Sir Francis Drake, who called in as he was sailing past. This first settlement had failed.

A Native American village set inside a fence designed to keep wild animals away.

Did you know… ?

- The settlers were well received by the Native Americans, and they allowed the English to build a fort and some cottages.
- Wherever the English had been, many Native American people started to die. Just as was happening to the **Aztecs** in the south, the English were bringing diseases for which the Native Americans had no immunity.

Q What happened soon after the English arrived?

Roanoke settlers vanish

The next year Raleigh sent a new expedition under John White (who was also an artist and whose illustrations you see on pages 16–17 and 22–23). It had 118 men, women and children. They reoccupied the Roanoke village.

There John White's daughter gave birth to the first English child to be born in North America. But when they arrived it was too late to plant crops and

John White feared the Native Americans would not trade, so he set off for England, planning a quick return trip. However, once in England all ships were needed as protection against the threat of a Spanish invasion (the Armada).

In fact it took three years before White was able to get enough money for the return journey. When he got there the settlement was empty. No one knows what happened to the settlers he left behind.

An artist's impression of Roanoke.

Did you know... ?

- Some of the colonists would have felt themselves superior to the natives and, since the natives were not Christians, would have felt justified in treating them badly.
- From trade, England learned of some foods and other products for the first time.
- Walter Raleigh is given the credit for introducing both tobacco and potatoes to Britain, although both of these were already known elsewhere in Europe from Spanish explorers.

Q **Why did some colonists treat the native peoples badly?**

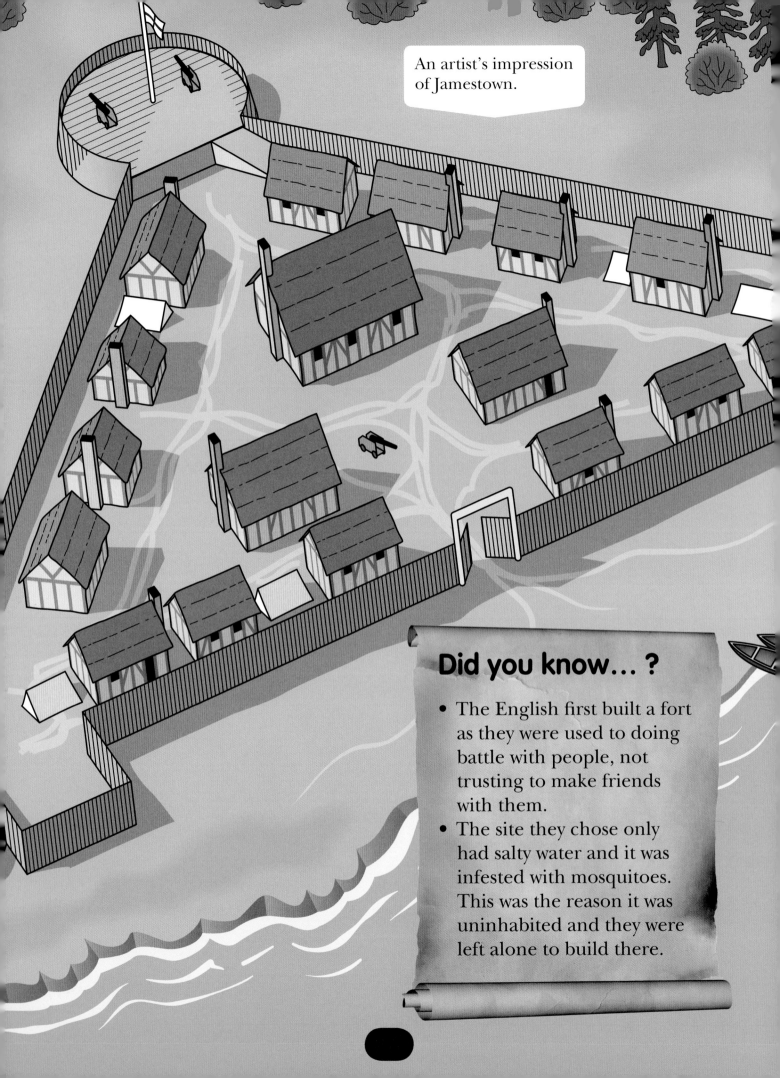

An artist's impression of Jamestown.

Did you know…?

- The English first built a fort as they were used to doing battle with people, not trusting to make friends with them.
- The site they chose only had salty water and it was infested with mosquitoes. This was the reason it was uninhabited and they were left alone to build there.

Jamestown

In June 1606, just three years after Elizabeth I died, King James I gave permission for a group of London merchants, called the Virginia Company, to start a trading post. By December, 108 settlers sailed from Plymouth with instructions to settle in Virginia.

When the ships arrived at Virginia, the settlers chose a site on the banks of the James River (they named it after the king). The settlement they named Jamestown.

Just like the people who had tried before them, the settlers soon ran into trouble trying to find enough food. For the first years the colony survived because of supplies brought from England. But the ships did not always arrive and the winter of 1609–1610 became known as the "starving time" because over eighty per cent of the town died of starvation.

Yet colonists kept coming, including those who finally made farming work. John Rolfe was the first man to produce a crop he could send back to England. That crop was Virginia tobacco. Rolfe soon made his fortune and this encouraged more people to travel to the area to plant tobacco. This time the colonists had succeeded and were there to stay.

 What was the first crop to be grown at Jamestown?

Growth of Plymouth population	
Date	Population
December, 1620	99
April, 1621	50
November, 1621	85
July, 1623	180
May, 1627	156
January, 1630	almost 300
January, 1643	approx. 2,000
January, 1691	approx. 7,000

Q Why did the Plymouth colony leave England?

Children dressing up at the reconstructed Plymouth Colony in the United States.

The Plymouth Colony

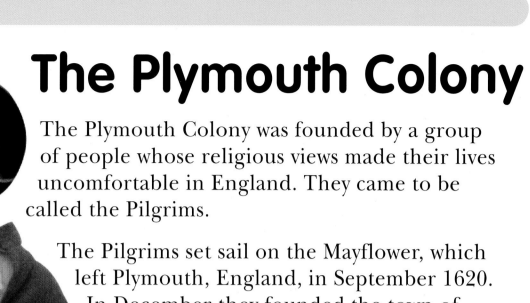

The Plymouth Colony was founded by a group of people whose religious views made their lives uncomfortable in England. They came to be called the Pilgrims.

The Pilgrims set sail on the Mayflower, which left Plymouth, England, in September 1620. In December they founded the town of Plymouth (near modern Boston).

All this time they were relying on stores they had brought with them. Then on 16 March, 1621, a Native American named Samoset, walked boldly into the midst of the settlement and proclaimed, "Welcome, Englishmen!". He had learned some English from fishermen who worked off the coast.

After terrible years when they nearly starved, the colonists were able to grow enough crops to feed themselves. At the end of the harvest, they thanked God for this. This event was what started the modern holiday of Thanksgiving, one of the most important days in the calendar of the United States.

Did you know... ?

- Europeans were running out of gold and one of the main reasons for going west was to find more gold.
- Peoples of the Americas traded in slaves before the Europeans arrived.
- When the Europeans arrived, they accidentally brought diseases that killed many Native Americans. The colonists needed to find workers for their **plantations**. The Portuguese were the first to bring slaves from Africa.

Cotton, which grows well in the warm, rainy climate of the southern USA.

Virginia tobacco leaves.

Q **What did the explorers bring back from the newly 'discovered' countries?**

Tudor exploration and modern times

The Tudor explorers found new routes to America and Asia and began new trade routes.

The explorers took many of the lands they visited from the people who had been living in them.

Slave trading was common throughout the world, as it had been from earliest times. But the new explorers began the movement of slaves from Africa to the Americas across the Atlantic.

The wealth from the lands the explorers reached added to the riches of Europe. With the money, new public buildings would be built, artists would flourish, and most people would find that life got better.

New foods such as cocoa, potatoes, sweet potatoes, tomatoes, squash and corn all came from the new lands.

Crops such as cotton and tobacco could be grown cheaply in the newly colonised areas (using slave labour) so that clothes got cheaper. Smoking became a popular past-time.

Potatoes and tomatoes are New World crops.

Glossary

Age of Discovery The time, starting in Portugal in the 1420s and ending about 200 years later, in which Europeans looking for gold, silver and spices, visited lands for the first time.

Aztec An important civilisation that lived in what is now Mexico.

ballast Heavy materials put in the bottom of a ship to help make the ship float upright.

booty Treasure captured from enemy ships.

colony/colonies A land ruled by another country.

convoy A group of ships that travel together for protection.

dysentery An infection that causes people to lose so much water that they die.

kayak A kind of canoe.

man o'war A ship designed to do battle, for example, galleons.

merchant A person who buys and sells goods to other traders.

plantation A very large farm growing just one type of crop. Plantations in the Age of Discovery were producing tobacco in Virginia.

privateer A person who set out to rob other people on behalf of his government.

slave trading The buying and selling of people.

Spanish Main The part of the sea off the coast of Spanish colonies.

Turks A historic term referring to Muslim peoples, the most powerful of whom were based in Turkey.

Index

Curriculum Visions

Curriculum Visions Explorers
This series provides straightforward introductions to key worlds and ideas.

You might also be interested in
Our slightly more detailed book, 'Tudor Age of Discovery'. There is a Teacher's Guide to match 'Tudor Age of Discovery'. Additional notes in PDF format are also available from the publisher to support 'Exploring the Tudor Age of Discovery'. All of these products are suitable for KS2.

Dedicated Web Site
Watch movies, see many more pictures and read much more in detail about the Tudors and Tudor exploration at:
www.curriculumvisions.com
(Professional Zone: subscription required)

A CVP Book
Copyright © 2007 Earthscape

The right of Brian Knapp to be identified as the author of this work has been asserted by him in accordance with the Copyright, Designs and Patents Act 1988.

Author
Brian Knapp, BSc, PhD

Educational Consultant
JM Smith (former Deputy Head of Wellfield School, Burnley, Lancashire)

Senior Designer
Adele Humphries, BA

Editor
Gillian Gatehouse

Photographs
The Earthscape Picture Library, except *The Granger Collection, New York* pages 18–19, 20–21; *ShutterStock* pages 1, 2–3, 30–31; *TopFoto* pages 4–5, 6–7, 8–9, 10–11, 12–13, 14–15, 16–17, 22–23, 28–29.

Illustrations
David Woodroffe except pages 24–25 *Mark Stacey*

Designed and produced by
Earthscape

Printed in China by
WKT Company Ltd

Exploring the Tudor Age of Discovery – *Curriculum Visions*
A CIP record for this book is available from the British Library
ISBN 978 1 86214 216 9

This product is manufactured from sustainable managed forests. For every tree cut down at least one more is planted.